GIRL, DO

A LIVING WORK

WOMEN EMPOWERMENT POETRY BOOK

PHOTOGRAPHY, POETRY, SPOKEN WORD AND STORIES SET TO ENCOURAGE AND INSPIRE.

ALICIA ROSEBUD

GirlDontGiveUp.com   ©2021   Girl, Don't Give Up

THIS BOOK IS DEDICATED TO WOMEN ALL OVER THE WORLD WHO HAVE EVER FELT LIKE THEY WERE NOT ENOUGH..
YOU ARE MORE THAN ENOUGH.
THIS IS YOUR TIME,
GIRL, DON'T GIVE UP.

ISBN: 9798480461343

TABLE OF CONTENTS

POETIC DEDICATIONS

I Saw You

I saw you, sitting at the table
and you stood up as I walked into the room
the roses in your hand couldn't hold a light, to
the love that would bloom. I saw you.

Like I have seen you, in every lifetime that we
have ever existed and it was like in an instant
my instincts kicked in
and there it was, what I have been missing.
I saw you.

And I knew that everything that has
happened, good or bad, up until this point and
time, has led me to the love of my life. And
everything makes sense, now, everything is
fine because,
I saw you.

That day, when finally, on the level that we are
in, I saw my best friend from generation to
generation. Standing there with open arms.
And a million lifetimes passed through my
mind, I will never forget the first time
I saw you.

My soul mate.

Thank you for always believing in me.
I love you.

A. Rosebud

My Hero

Girl,
YOU DON'T GIVE UP.
You are an inspiration.
You fight for what you love,
you don't let ANYONE take it.

You are the rock of your family,
and the heart of your home.
The life of the party,
the queen on her throne.

You worked hard
to be who you are.
You didn't have
a head start,
and you were dealt
shitty cards-
but you played them-
strategically-
and look at you now.
The type of woman,
to make her
ancestors proud.
You are my hero.

-A. Rosebud

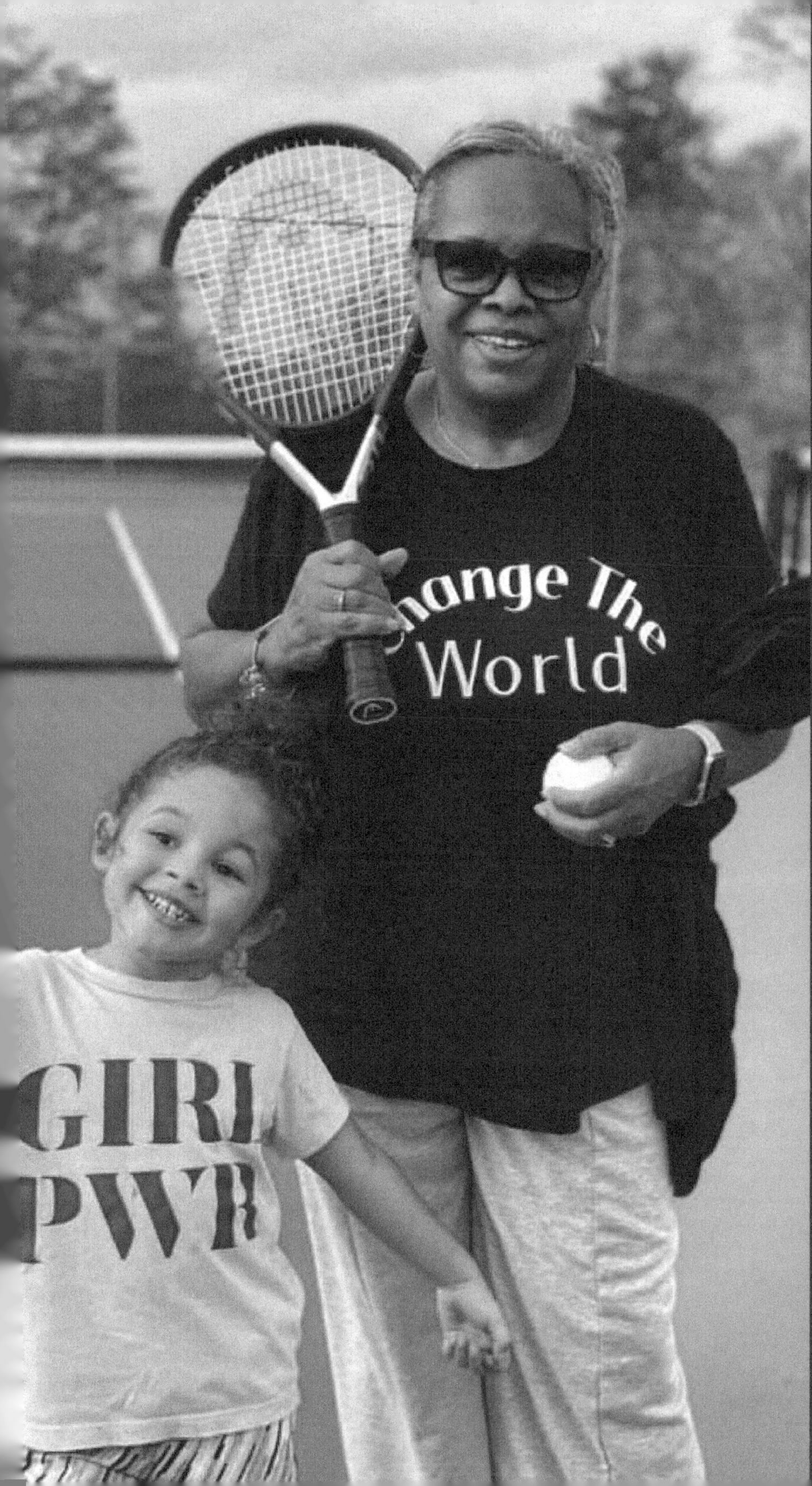
World
GIRL
PWR

They Call The Wind-Mariya

Understand, my sweet child,
NOTHING is impossible.
Believe in the materialization
of your biggest hopes and dreams.
You are a symbol of PEACE.
Your light is UNSTOPPABLE.
Your grace has enlightened my life,
and brightend my eyes.
Your heart shines so bright,
you are like the SUN and
the earth needs you,
to inspire the heavens,
the way you have inspired me.
Girl, that energy-
I love you so much.
I'm so proud to be your mom.

-A. Rosebud

Maci,

Girl, don't give up-
be resilient and don't let anyone
turn down your brilliance,
make their eyes adjust.
Sure- pay it forward but
first they are going to have
to buy your trust.
Just know
in life- there's
A time for peace.
A time for war.
A time for love and
your voice will never be
too little to lift hers up.
You are going to change the world.
I just know it.
Don't stop growing.
I love you girl.

-A. Rosebud

To my Dad,

Thank you for always giving the shirt off of your back to make sure I was okay growing up. Thank you for the years of hard work, dedication, practices, sports, academics and room to grow. Thank you for teaching me patience, work ethic, manners, and morals. Thanks for rolling up your sleeves and doing anything you can to help me achieve my dreams. You have inspired me to be the person I am today in so many ways. I just couldn't thank you enough for all that you do. I pray that I can repay you in your lifetime.
I love you so much!

To my Father in Law,

Thank you for putting your family first and for making sure we never go without. You have a huge heart and you are always looking for ways to help. I want you to know that everything you do for us is so appreciated. Thank you for raising my husband to be the stand up man that he is. You are an inspiration and an incredible human being. We are so blessed to have you in our lives. I love you!

To my sons,

I love you boys so much. You both are so absolutely incredible in your own way. I pray that as you grow, you never forget to use your manners, open doors for others, lend a helping hand and volunteer as much as possible. I pray that you will be the type of men that do the dirty work and the dishes without a complaint. The kind of men to make sure home is always taken care of and your family feels loved. I believe in you both so much. I can't wait to see all you become.

Love, Mom.

INTRODUCTION AND INSPIRATION

Okay, so I guess since you purchased a copy of my book, I should probably let you in a little closer than I usually allow people to get into my life....

Trauma dump in 3 2 1.

I am going to be honest with you, right now, in this very moment, I have no idea where my life is going or what is going to happen next. I feel like everything is completely falling apart or perhaps it is all coming together, I am really not sure. Lately, I have found myself searching for my purpose and losing a grip on the reality of just how special the journey is. Life is hard and it is so easy to get caught up in doubt and fear of the unknown.

This past year and a half has somehow been both heaven and hell for me. Finding the will to go on is a huge challenge when your happiness and what you believe to be your purpose has been robbed from you and it wasn't your own fault, but who can you really blame?

You see- on the first day of the shut downs- at the beginning of the pandemic, my husband found me on the bathroom floor having an asthma induced seizure. Anxiety is what ultimately triggered my asthma attack, which has happened 100 times before, but not like this. I'd get anxiety, I would cry and then I would calm down, use my inhaler, focus on breathing and snap out of it-but not this time. This time was different. I just wanted to die. That is it. I couldn't stop crying. I couldn't catch my breath. I just couldn't get these terrible thoughts out of my head of what it would feel like if I just got ran over by a bus, or fell from the window of a sky scrapper. I just didn't want to do this thing called life anymore. I couldn't get these thoughts out of my head. I would have flashbacks to the day I saw my own mother face down, dead on the floor of her apartment, and how all of her problems ended that day. I hit myself in my head with the palm of my hand like that would actually erase the memories of these haunting thoughts. But they were still there and I just kept crying.

I guess I hyperventilated because I couldn't get ahold of my breathing and the oxygen stopped traveling to my brain. I collapsed to the floor and the muscles in my toes, hands and lips began to tighten. Before I could call for help, the words were gone and as hard as I tried, I couldn't even let out a whisper- let alone a cry for help. My husband was in the other room, but would he realize there was something wrong before it was too late? I was terrified and as much as I wanted to die in that moment, I didn't want to go out like that. My kids needed me still.

It all started when we had the government mandated shut downs related to the coronavirus pandemic. The state had shut down our businesses because entertainment was not essential. This wasn't the first time our state made it hard to operate our business, but this is the first time we were completely out of control and had no say so whatsoever on when we could open again. We had just invested ALL of our savings from a decade of 100 hour work weeks and dedication to our business and customers. We had finally built up a solid team and our company was growing exponentially. We had just signed 3 new leases with plans to open 3 more entertainment venues. We had just closed on our first franchise sale and reinvested that money back into our business model. Our business was BOOMING and it was absolutely glorious. Until it wasn't.

The pandemic changed all of our lives- differently. I guess the hardest part for me was this little reminder that there are so many people or entities that have power over me and that is so frustrating. I felt like my freedom was taken. My freedom to work and feed my family. I still felt the pain in my hands and my back from the labor of building this empire that we put our heart and souls into- only to be told that we would have to close our doors- for an undisclosed amount of time- to help the greater good- and we did that. We were compliant, we increased our cleaning procedures, we limited our business to 50% capacity, we stayed stocked with PPE, sanitizer, gloves, and masks to have available for our guest and we closed our doors for a total of 6 months in Pennsylvania- (4 months in the beginning and then another 2 months starting in December, 2020 for the second wave) for the greater good.

We told our customers they would need to wear masks- because our governor mandated it- and we LOST nearly 50% of our customers who were just unwilling to support a business that required masks. I get it-people don't like to be told what to do, but I took it super personal. I spent so much time building relationships with my customers and that was just something I didn't understand. I guess all of those years of dedicating our lives to our customers, staying late, all of the discounts, the freebies, the fundraising, the time, money and effort I spent, meant nothing. That is when I realized that my customers didn't view me as a person but as a service and that harsh reality HURT. I thought these people were my friends but as soon as I didn't have a service to offer to them, people stopped caring and began gossiping about me and my family. I just wanted to give up.

I explained to my customers that this wasn't political- we just didn't want to be responsible for life lost- so we just did what we thought was right at the time- which was to listen to our local government and follow CDC guidelines. After laboring for the past two months to close a few of our venues for good and then tearing down a few venues for relocation- I look back and wander- did we make the right choices during the pandemic? I still think so..but I do believe we had to pay a huge price to keep our customers and staff safe. From our choices- none of our staff got COVID from work. None of our customers got COVID from our tournaments or leagues- and our parents made it to through the thick of it until they could be vaccinated. No lives were lost in our care and I think that means something. To be completely honest with you- I think we would have lost 50% of our customers if we would have not required people to wear masks and people may have died from our choices. The reality is that you can't really make everyone happy and in times of great stress and despair, when the people are divided, as a leader and an entrepreneur, you just have to do what you think is right. Your true friends and supporters will still be there.

Truthfully our industry was overlooked when it came to funding. We lost nearly 75% of our gross sales in 2020 from all of the mandates and shutdowns- and we were able to access a supplement of around 10% of that with PPP loans that were issued to help with payroll and rent. My husband and I completely lost our salary with our own company. That was hard and the harsh reality of, needing to close or relocate, began to kick in after the government asked our industry to shut down again in December of 2020.

We came from little means, and grew our company to a national franchise in the entertainment industry. This was huge, we worked HARD to get where we were. Finally we began to become lenders instead of borrowers. Finally we saw a break. Finally we got to sit down at the table to eat the cake instead of serving it- and before we could take a bite- the dinner was over.

We held out for a year and a half. We did everything we could. The stress we were going through began to take a toll on our marriage and we were blaming each other for everything. We went back to working 100 hour work weeks- in the face of the pandemic and we were stretched thin. There was a revolving door of new hires and staffing has been an issue due to the accessibility of unemployment compensation and the severity of the pandemic at times. We just couldn't continue to grow in this industry, in this area- so we took a few of our businesses out back and shot them.

I think I saw this coming on day one of the shut down. I saw our livelihood and everything that we worked so hard for being taken from us. I think that is how I ended up laying on my bathroom floor, gasping for what was almost my last breath.
After the ambulance arrived and the reality of what had just happened, hit me, I changed. My eyes opened up and there were these little voices who kept saying, "Mommy, I am so happy you are alive." My husband hugged me and said "I don't know what I would ever do without you." God, that broke my heart and at the same time, healed it. I almost left my babies that day. Like my mom left me when I was a child. Maybe not in the same way- but I can't imagine ever inflicting that type of pain on them. I felt completely helpless. It was the worst feeling I have ever felt.

I am not really sure what we are going to do next or where exactly we will go from here but I know that whatever it is, it will be so much better than I could have imagined. I thank GOD that I am here today to experience the struggle so that I can embrace triumph once again. I decided to stop living for the happiness of everyone else and to dig deep inside to figure out what is most fulfilling to me and I think I have. I am most happy when I am writing, creating, marketing, throwing axes and with my family- at the beach. So that is where I am going to start and time will tell where this road takes us.

One thing I know for certain- reading the stories of all of the brave women who submitted a photo for this book to happen has saved my morale throughout this really difficult time in our lives. It has given me new life. It reminded me that everyone has their own story to tell and if you listen, we are all much more alike than we are different.

I hope this book encourages you to live your best life. I hope these words and these photos can make you feel, less alone. I hope we can inspire you, to stay strong and face your problems head on. Girl, don't give up.

A. Rosebud

To the contributors on this book.

I just want to say thank you so much to all of the women who submitted a photo and their story to make this possible. It has been my absolute pleasure to read about what you have been through, to reflect on your story and your photo and to write poetry about you.

Each and every one of you have such an inspiring story to tell and I am honored that you have allowed me to share it in a way that can be healing for so many other women who might be going through something similar. Thank you to all of the women who have submitted their own written works in the trauma dump section of this book. You are so brave for sharing, and I just can't stop thanking you, so much, from the bottom of my heart. Together, we could really reach so many women who just need some reassurance that they are not alone.

To everyone who reads this, I hope this book inspires you to live your best life, to be all you were meant to be and to reach for your dreams!

-A. Rosebud

PICTURES
AND
POETRY OF
EMPOWERING WOMEN

THIS POEM IS A SELF REFLECTION.

Like Silver, She is in the fire.

The world doesn't deserve her
but she gives it her all-
none the less.
People will desert her
but she still wishes
them- the best.
Her own family will hurt her
feels like a knife
to the chest.

People see her and think
"she's a queen,
she's a boss babe.
She makes it look easy"
but she's -exhausted.

She hustles hard
and she grinds to get by.
It's a dollar for her efforts,
but they offer a dime.
She knows she'll
change the world,
It's just a matter of time,
So she takes
what she can get
while she's being refined.

She might be in the fire
but God's not done with her yet.
He keeps his eye on her
until he sees his,
reflect.

She keeps her faith strong
while she's taking her test.
One thing is for certain,
God is leading her steps.

-A. Rosebud

Never Say Die

She wears her heart
on her sleeve,
in fear she may
regret it, if
she doesn't get
that sentence in-
she may never
get the chance.
That is separation- anxiety -
disguised as high demand,
for a confirmation,
that you won't leave her.
You say you won't,
because you "love her"
but so did her mother.
Those thoughts haunt her,
"am I enough?" whispers across
the back of her neck-
she loses her breath
and takes a few steps
before she sits down.
She raises her head
from her hands,
with fire in her eyes,
she stares straight
at the devil like,
"Wouldn't you love it,
if I quit now?"

-A. Rosebud

THIS POEM IS INSPIRED BY JESSICA SULLIVAN.

She'll Take You Through A Loop

she is unique
and cannot be confined
like a jade vine.
Her beauty is rare,
don't you dare
stop to stare-
she is bold and she will ask-
"what the hell are you looking at?"
With one hand on her hip
and another on her-
axe.
"You're gonna have
to pay for that."
She'll laugh-
(in her head
she knows she needs
to break that)
because
she is
dead
ass
serious
and you should
run away but
she is stunning and
you're a little bit
-curious-
what does she mean?
Now you are caught
in her -energy,
with no release
because

-A. Rosebud

THIS POEM IS INSPIRED BY CHRISTINA SIMS.

Born to Rule

Girl,
You are on fire.
Your soul radiates elegance
and burns bright
from the flames that ignite,
the queen within you.
You were never meant
to work for someone else-
you were born to rule.

You leave a trail
of wisdom
everywhere you go.
You are special,
but I think you have
always known

-deep within you.

Because,
anytime,
anyone,
anywhere
would think otherwise,
-you figured out a way
to remind them-
you wear the crown,
and yes, queen,
it fits you so well.

-A. Rosebud

THIS POEM IS INSPIRED BY RACHEL MILLER.

Exhibit A

You knew she wasn't ordinary,
so you tried to keep her -to yourself.
Like your home was a shelter,
so she didn't end up on a shelf
of some museum that didn't
gain your approval first.
You knew she was valuable,
but you concealed -her worth.
You spoon-fed her crumbs of life
so that she didn't starve.
Dressed her wounds after you stabbed
her in the heart.
Hoping she wouldn't find the light,
you left her in the dark,
cut off from the world
so no one could see her scars.
While you were
sound asleep, she would lie awake,
thinking about the ways
she could escape,
until one day-
she finally did.
She discovered
her strength-within.
Turns out, she's a warrior,
with the will to live.
An amazing mother to both of her kids,
Worthy of the best life has to give-
and if she has to fight for it,
well then,
that's what it is-
but she will never be held
captive again.
-A. Rosebud

Like a Phoenix

Does her boldness offend you?
The way she delegates a room
and operates like a fine tuned
machine- to get the job done.
While you twiddle your thumbs
and say "she's so dumb."
Pace the room again and think,
it's time to buzz, catch a buzz
-now you are buzzed,
look at her-she's the one-
you're so in love.
But then she speaks.
"Fuuuuck.......why did she have to
think for herself?" You think to yourself.
before you cut her off....
"Shhhhhhhhhhhhhhhhhh!"
all you want is for her to be- quiet,
she's so opinionated
and that triggers your-violence. "SILENCE!
Why can't you just be SILENT?!"

Doors slam, door jams and hearts are broken.
She had been crying out for years
you never noticed.
Same words, different tears
clouding her focus and keeping her near.

But one day she, LEFT. Seeking appreciation
when all you had to do was speak words of
affirmation....Do you have- regrets?

Thinking back to the life you once built
after it crashes
like a house of cards, now it is ashes
and she rose up like a phoenix
because she always does.
Her family taught her how to love,
but you took that for granted.
She's gave you so
many chances, damn it.

-A. Rosebud

THIS POEM IS INSPIRED BY LACEY DOUDS.

<u>If They Could See You Now</u>

No one ever prepares you
for the loss of your parents
and the kind of emptiness it leaves,
somewhere deep inside of your chest
that makes it hard to breathe.
All you really want to do is sleep,
praying for them to be there
in your dreams,
to just give you some... guidance.
And sometimes they are,
when you listen
in the midst of the silence,
while everything is quiet,
a woman walks by and
smells of your mom's perfume,
she turns around and winks at you,
her husband runs along behind
and you think- is that dad too?
You know that they are there
but you can't touch them, or hug them,
and that's the sad truth.
Life is hard without your parents,
but take a look at you.
Wouldn't they be so proud
of the mother, wife and woman
that you grew into?
I know I am. I look up to you.
I love the way your smile,
lights up the room.
Your work ethic, your drive,
you are unstoppable.
You are smart and you are kind,
you are responsible.
You are the type of woman,
to do the impossible,
You are golden, girl.

-A. Rosebud

THIS POEM IS INSPIRED BY CHELSEA COLANGELO-TOLA

You Are Powerful

You know who you are,
and you always have,
deep in your soul.
Your energy would
cause a heart attack,
if it wasn't so cold.
Step into that power,
darling, you are
meant to rule.
Whatever you want
you can have it, don't get
comfortable.
Keep on going,
keep on growing,
keep on finding yourself.
Eat, sleep and breathe clean,
keep an eye
on your health.
Manifest your dreams and
build on your wealth.
Sometimes all you can do is
rely on yourself.
So be there for you
and one day you can be all
that you ever needed,
for somebody else.

-A. Rosebud

THIS POEM IS INSPIRED BY ANDREA MORGAN.

Unrealistic Standards

Social media can be
like a demon
causing you to see -it-
instead of yourself in the mirror-
it's -deceiving.

These platforms will
make you crazy,
and you'll keep on believing
you aren't enough-
and you are not complete if
you don't have -lip fillers
or double Ds.
I mean,
How skinny should a girl be
before she is perceived to be
on drugs, anorexic
or unhealthy?
It's a disease-
comparing yourself to these
-unrealistic standards-

We need to break free
from our own thoughts.
At the end of the day,
if you saw, what I saw,
Girl, you would know
YOU-ARE-HOT.

-A. Rosebud

THIS POEM IS INSPIRED BY KIM HAMRICK.

Angel On Earth

There is a special seat saved in heaven
for people who lift up others,
in the midst of their sorrow.
Who make you thankful for today
and take away
the stressors of tomorrow.

I hope you know that your smile
brings hope to all who see it.
Your soul shines so bright
I just couldn't believe it.
The first time I saw your light,
I wandered how you achieved it.
After hearing your story,
I think you received it.

I think that God chose you
to be an angel on Earth.
Perhaps, when your mother passed,
she put in the word.
I think that you have a purpose
that you are ready to serve,
and whatever you were called to do,
you have already heard.

Keep on going girl, you are ready.
Don't give up, when those wings get
heavy,
chin up and coast -until you feel steady.
God will be your guide, if you'll just let him.

-A. Rosebud

THIS POEM IS INSPIRED BY DANA BROWN.

That Girl

That girl knows her worth
and she would never
settle for less.
If she ever loved you,
that girl gave you her best.
She kept her chin up
and demanded respect.
And if you messed with that girl,
then she got up and left.

That girl came so
far on her own.
Raising two sons,
with the right to her throne.
She reaps her own harvests
from the seeds that she's sown,
but even a true queen
gets tired of being alone.

God didn't want her
to be suffering.
It's only right that
he would send her a king
to get down on one knee
and give her a ring,
That girl right there,
she deserves every thing.

I am so glad you found it.
-A. Rosebud

THIS POEM IS INSPIRED BY HEATHER POLLINS.

You are Wonder Woman

Darling, you are worth so much more
than the finest emeralds and gold.
Don't be fooled.

Diamonds are formed under pressure,
and baby, they have nothing on you.
This is true.

Your soul glistens like the sun,
and your eyes are striking in a way
that means business
and pleasure at the same time.

You are comfort, you are home,
and you are peace,
You are strength, you are hope,
and you are relief.
But who are these things to you?

As you grow into the woman
you are meant to be,
I want you to remember
this one thing...
You can't pour from
an empty cup.
–find a way to fill yours up.

-A. Rosebud

There is NO Shortcut To Success.

It is never too late to become
The person you
are meant to be,
You see, she
was buried deep within
and the only way to reach her
was to dig through
your own mistakes,
to live out your own fate.

No one could
do that for you.
Perhaps they could
offer a helping hand,
or maybe a bit of advice,
but this is YOUR life.

And girl,
YOU are in control.
So hit your goals,
trust your soul,
and don't be fooled.

You are a boss, babe.

-A. Rosebud

THIS POEM IS INSPIRED BY JENNIFER GRUNDY.

Shedding Judgements

Watching you transform
is amazing,
but it is not just the weight
that I see you losing,
it's so much more.
In your eyes,
I see so much happiness,
genuine happiness
for the first time.
I could cry.
I must admit,
I have always thought,
you are one of the most
beautiful people on earth.
Inside and out.
There's just something about,
YOU.
I've always looked up to you
as a symbol of beauty,
I wander your skincare routine,
I wish my lashes looked like yours,
your smile is perfect.
Perhaps I should have
said this more
but the -truth is,
I too felt insecure.
Why do we do this to ourselves?
I hope you know that you
deserve to be loved.
In every single way,
you are beautiful,
a true gift from above,
and even on your worst day,
-you are perfect.

-A. Rosebud

THIS POEM IS INSPIRED BY STEPHANIE FRANKS-HELWICH

<u>Your Future Is Bright</u>

I want you to forget
where you came from
and remember who you are.
You have come so far.

Everyone who has ever
tried to bring you down,
was already below you,
and now they'll never know YOU.

Keep on going and don't look back
there is nothing left for you there,
your value is rare.
Don't you forget that.

Only let people in- who care,
You will know them
by their frequency,
don't you drop to theirs.

If you knew where you were going,
you would be dancing in the streets.
Keep your head up and stay focused
as you become-
all you were meant to be,
now that you are free.
-A. Rosebud

THIS POEM IS INSPIRED BY SAMILAH SANCHEZ.

You Might Have To Fight

Your voice is powerful,
and you are not afraid to use it.
You were 9 years old,
starting a movement.
You can't be told,
"You can't do it."
You'll turn around
and do it
-three times-
You found your drive
standing in the heat
in long lines
holding picket signs
just for a chance to see
your dad once a week
and that shit wasn't fair
but he-
got through it.
And so did you.
That changed your outlook,
of what you can handle,
now look at you.
What ever you are up against,
has already lost.
You are the boss,
you come out on top,
and you won't be stopped.

-A. Rosebud

THIS POEM IS INSPIRED BY RACHEL REED.

Powerful Woman

When I look at you,
I can feel your power.
Girl, you are connected.
You know what you want,
and you know who you are,
when looking at your reflection.
Your soul vibrates and operates
on another dimension
and anything you want,
you manifest it.
You will cut off anyone
who doubts you, ghosts you
or makes you feel rejection.
You have dreams to chase
and moves to make.
Girl, you are respected.
You live your life,
and chase your dreams
and you don't let
anything come between.
This is your life
this is your movie
this is your scene.
You are beautiful,
at peace
and happy.
You are free.

-A. Rosebud

There is so much left for you.

While the other kids
were getting ready for school,
you were in a doctors office,
at 8 years old,
hearing a diagnosis
that would shake your soul.
Making you question
whether or not, you should
make real goals.
Your mental health and self worth
began to take a toll.
You forgot to love yourself first,
you became emotional.
Gave yourself to a man,
who made you feel like
you had no control.
You had to become
a young mom,
but you stepped up and
NAILED- that role.
Ditched the guy,
who made you cry.
and said, "Fuck that fool."
You went to therapy and you
gained some self control.
You seeked God,
began to pray,
and you healed your soul.
Now you are married
with two children
and your heart is full.
If your life is the newspaper,
this bit, is just an article.
You have so much
to look forward to
and you deserve it,
you heave a heart of gold.
-A. Rosebud

You Saw The Light

You were told you weren't
good enough,
for most
of your life.
That you weren't
thin enough, smart enough,
or even nice.
I bet this made loving yourself
a fight,
I bet you were losing sleep
at night,
wandering if they were right....
But then
one day you saw the light
in the dark,
and it opened your eyes.
You understood that
through the lens,
you can, capture time.
But true beauty
is what you found
when you stood on the other side.
It's crazy how quick
life can change when you frequent
another vibe.

–A. Rosebud

THIS POEM IS INSPIRED BY JANNELLE LONG.

COMPLETED

Imagine this, your phone rings,
you're with your husband and
you put it on speaker.
You find out - about - two baby girls,
they are malnourished, anemic,
and having seizures.
They need parents, they need a home,
someone to love them,
-they need a teacher-
I guess you don't have to imagine it,
because God already called you
-to be her-
You see,
he could have picked anyone
but he chose you
to be their mom.
Now when it rains,
through the storm,
you are their calm.
You are there to comfort
and protect them from- anyone-
You would never let
anything hurt them,
you wont desert them.
You'll listen first and
they will feel like
you've heard them.
You made it your mission to serve them,
because they are your world.
You'll make sure they feel valued
and as they grow,
they will know that they are
your baby girls.
-You are complete now.

-A. Rosebud

Going Up

As a child, you were lost,
with no one to lead you.
You looked up to your mom,
but she would mistreat you,
and then leave you.
You saw your father behind bars,
that shit would eat you.
Surrounded by toxic people
who would cheat you.
You were still a child yourself,
and you had to feed two.
You stayed with abusive men,
because you felt the need to.
One failed relationship
after another,
struggling with your purpose
and being a mother.
Felt like you were cursed
and made to suffer.
That shit hurt,
but you grew tougher
and built upon your bond
with God.
Now look at you,
it's like you were made new
and now you are not afraid to
chase your dreams –
because no one can persuade you
behind the scenes
to come down to their level.
You have come so far,
-don't let up-
Keep your faith in God,
Keep your head up
Girl,
it's about to get a
whole lot better!

-A. Rosebud

You Changed

Your smile lights up the party
like the sun lights up the sky.
You are diamond in the rough,
and the apple of the eye,
of everyone who meets you.
Your soul shines like the lights
on the streets -you-
changed-
but only in the best way.
Your confidence is
on Beyonce'
on her best day.
I LOVE THAT ABOUT YOU
and I am HERE FOR IT.
Sitting down, sipping tea,
clapping my hands.
I WILL CHEER FOR IT.
You are everything
that makes up a woman,
Girl, you are a treat.
You are the full course
plus desert,
Bon Appétit
Eat your heart out, make you hurt,
"if you fuck with me
or one of my sisters."
You are a pistol,
and you have already shot
all of the doubt
that anyone has ever had-
that girl is ALL WOMAN,
and that WOMAN is
BAD.

-A. Rosebud

THIS POEM IS INSPIRED BY KATI TEREK.

<u>Good-Grief</u>
<u>TW: Pregnancy Loss</u>
Passions burning
from the kind of love that makes you want to procreate
-a few weeks pass,
now your period is late.
You tell your husband, and he is on his way.
You grab a test and it feels like it takes
an hour but it's a minute's wait
before it states-
that you are- pregnant.
This is great and you celebrate
-with a date.
You start picking names.
You come up with a way to- announce it.
Maybe during Christmas, when everyone's in town.
Your whole life changes and everything surrounds it.
but before your blessing has been counted,
the devil pounces, taking your baby
and every ounce of safety,
you once felt.
You feel vulnerable inside,
you get the "Why am I?"
the "What did I do?"
the "Did I deserve this?"
You blame yourself-you cry for help-
but it's like no body heard it-
but then you found a tribe
of couples who have experienced
the same serpent.
You found a platform
to release all of that hurt and pain.
Now, look at your strength
It is incredible the way you stand up in the face
of pregnancy loss for others to say-
"things will get better,
you will be okay."
I think that is such a beautiful way,
-to be.
I think that is good grief.
-A. Rosebud

THIS POEM IS INSPIRED BY SAMANTHA WEINER.

A Time For Change

Closure is all you needed.
An explanation, a reason.
"Why are you leaving?"
You would scream it,
and nothing in return.
Ghosted, left to burn,
that shit hurt.
But that same fire,
meant to kill you–
set you off.
With no explanation
for what went wrong
you changed the tune
to every song
that made you.
Now you will never
let another man break you.
This was your breakthrough.

-A. Rosebud

When you want something done right...

That girl fixes shit,
and gets it done.
She builds relationships,
yes- she's the one-
who built an entire network,
where there wasn't one,
just to network,
her business some,
in a new city
where she wasn't from.
She's a genius,
can't you see it,
the way she
creates the
dreams that
make life seem
appealing
for more people
then just her self.
The kind of girl
to build
generational wealth.

-A. Rosebud

Military Wife Life

You are inspiring.
The way you raise
your children and awareness
for our country,
while your husband protects it.
Girl, you are perfection.
Seeds of hope
were sown from your hands
when you introduced
The BB Military Wife Life collection.
And isn't that just like you?
To bring people together
to make them feel connected.
I've read your blog,
and I love your growth,
keep on going,
and keep on daring
to be different.

You are gifted.

-A. Rosebud

Girl, I Love You

You don't know how many times,
that smile or words from your kind
heart to mine, have stopped my crying,
my dear friend.
You pour into others cups so much
you forgot to leave yours open.
You are like sunshine in the wintertime,
that melts snow from the driveway.
You brighten the day
of anyone who encounters you,
unless they look at you sideways.
You are like fire and ice
sugar and spice
you are angry and nice
at the same damn time.
GIRL, I LOVE YOU
and all that you have been through
has shaped you.
You are perfect,
you are worth it.
Health, wealth, love and happiness-
you deserve it.
You have earned it.

-A. Rosebud

THIS POEM IS INSPIRED BY KIRSTIE CORTAZZO.

All is Right

Hope is born when
you get down on
your hands and knees
and beg God
to change your life
but before you can
stand up–
the hair on
the back of
your neck does
and you know that
things are about to
shift into your favor.
Because GOD
became involved–
wrongs are about
to be made right.
The grey area
will become
black and white–
–clear as day,
true as night,
God will make a way,
where there is
no path in sight,
like he brought back
the love of your life.
All is right.
Your future is bright.

-A. Rosebud

THIS POEM IS INSPIRED BY CIERRA CARPENTER.

Let Your Guard Down

They might seem fragile,
but you better handle them with care.
Like glass –they will cut you,
if you drop them.

They ended up abused–
in all of their relationships,
and they thought that–
they were the problem.

So trusting you, is an issue.
It's not personal,
its just that is something
that robs them.

You see, sometimes they
put up a guard so high,
that they forget it's there,
and they can't see anyone,
so they think nobody cares,
which is fair
–and valid.
But if they knew,
just how many people
look up to them,
they would be astounded.

–A. Rosebud

Two Feet On The Ground

You don't know how
strong you can be until
being strong is your only option.
With a broken foot,
you managed to walk away
from a love that was toxic.
Packed up and moved
17 years worth of building
-your life- in boxes.

At the time it felt like forever,
but it was only a moment,
before you were settled
in to your new home and
getting ready for
Christmas.
With two kids,
you managed to
check off their
wish list.
You did it.

By spring, you were walking
with two feet on the ground.
A smile on your face and
your head in the clouds.
nothing could break you,
or bring you down.
You were no longer bound.

Finally- you chose YOU,
and I think it was about time
somebody did.

-A. Rosebud

Shelter From The Storm

Life for you was never easy,
it wasn't like something
you would see
on a TV.
It was REAL.

You went through
some shit,
that would give,
even a soldier, chills.
Your skin became thick
but your mind was ill.
A constant cycle of
anxious thoughts
and time to kill,
so you would
medicate to
numb the pain-
you didn't want
to feel.....
It's easy to get
comfortable.
But you didn't.
You pulled yourself out of it.
You reached deep down in your
soul and found
something to live for,
something to die for,
something to try for.
now you are clean,
a wife and a mother of 4.
Your mind is no longer at war,
the sun is shinning,
life is good
You found a shelter
from your storm .

-A. Rosebud

THIS POEM IS INSPIRED BY ALICIA CLIFFORD.

Supreme

You set your
intentions on
self love,
and
now we are
all under
your spell.
Your beauty is
from above
but you got your fire
from hell –
you fought through
it to get here,
you were never
one to dwell.
You made it out alive–
with a soul
you wouldn't sell.
You found your
inner child,
your power
and all that
you can be.
Whatever your
heart desires,
you will live out
your dreams.
You will have it all,
you will succeed.
They would kill
to see you fall
but now you are
SUPREME–
You know
what that
means.

-A. Rosebud

<u>Sono Essence</u>

You knew what it was like
for your confidence to suffer,
over something you
couldn't cover-
skin imperfections,
you hid under.

This made it really
hard to find yourself.
You would look in the mirror
and see someone else.
Happiness is a mindset
that you hadn't felt.

For 11 years you struggled,
and couldn't find something
on the shelf- to help.
So you made it yourself.

You connected
Mind + Body + Spirit
to heal from within.
Empowering others,
to love their skin.

<u>Sono Essence</u>

inspired by
Mind + Body + Spirit Connection.
and the love of holistic living.
Finally something that works,
something effective.
Finally, somebody did it.

-A. Rosebud

THIS POEM IS INSPIRED BY TERRI ANDERSON.

Damn Girl,

It looks good on you,
the way you have stepped
into your own.
You decided that you are
no longer willing,
to give up your throne
to serve
somebody else.
Because-
you deserve to be served
-yourself.
Never again,
will you change
or conform
to a lesser version of you,
to make others feel more-
comfortable.
You are no longer,
vulnerable.
Seats in your life are only
reserved for people
you deem
honorable.
That is peace.
You have made it.
Now you are
unstoppable.

-A. Rosebud

Plot Twist

Isn't it funny how
every time we try
to plan out our lives,
there's a plot twist.
You covered all
of your bases
but you forgot it's
-not your game-
and God had
another calling
upon your name.
So you listened.
You took a step back
from your vision.
Eventually,
you went back
for your degree,
and life was different,
but once again,
you had to
make another
life changing decision
and this time
you just didn't
-agree with it.
But you didn't
have a say because of
the amount of money
that you made.
So what did you do...
You increased your value.
Now, no one
can talk down to you.
You are wiser than most,
and if someone
ever tries you, you'll say-
"The Hell I Won't"

-A. Rosebud

THIS POEM IS INSPIRED BY AMANDA EVANS.

Waterfall

Sometimes love isn't
all that it is
cracked up to be.
Loving the wrong person
will mess with
your energy
and rob you
of your inner peace.
Have you looking
in the mirror like,
"what's wrong with me?"
The truth is,
we are all a little crazy.
But that kind of fire,
is what it takes
to be amazing-
and you are nothing
short of that.
So surround yourself
with people who are
in support of that
and don't look back,
because
that's not where
you are going.
Don't be afraid to love
because,
you know it
was never your fault,
after all.
Feel everything you can,
right now in this moment,
like you felt this,
waterfall.

-A. Rosebud

THIS POEM IS INSPIRED BY CHRISTIANA SCHULTZ.

Endless Love

Fortunately and
unfortunately,
the truth is-
our lives can change
any second-
and you were
hit -head on
unexpected.
Your challenges
have been endless.
You felt disconnected,
you lost your dog
and then your job
from the pandemic.
Your pain from the accident
became-systemic.
Just when you thought,
you wanted to end it-
there she was,
you found a friend
with endless -love.
On your worst days,
she calms you.
On your best days,
the bonds true.
If you ever think
about giving up,
she reminds you
that- you are enough.
You are needed.
You are wanted.
You are loved.

-A. Rosebud

You are- like Paris,
the first week of October.
Fashion week,
when you hit the runway,
it's over-
because you are
the star of the show.
Sometimes I wander,
if you even know,
just how absolutely
beautiful, you are.
Sure, you will grow
and one day become,
all you were meant to be,
but right here,
right now,
in this moment,
you are,
perfectly-
imperfect.
Your beauty is
so much deeper
than the surface.
Sometimes you
seem a little
bit nervous,
but as soon
as you speak-
you do the world
a service.
It's like we already know,
that whatever
you are about to say,
will brighten our day.
Don't let the world change
-you.

-A. Rosebud

HAH!

Oh, you tried to mess with her?!
-Youuuu tried to mess with her?
Hah!

That girl makes the devil
scurry back to hell
when the sun rises.
That girl shows up late
because the show doesn't start
until she arrives and
you thought -you would
take -her- down?!

HAH.
Step aside, sit down.
It's time for a lesson...
You see that girl
allowed for you to have
everything that you have,
she -was- a- blessing -

and you took advantage
of her- clown.
You make me laugh.
HAH!
But it wasn't funny
for her, now
was it?

You made her
fear for her life,
you're disgusting
now you are just
specs of nothing-

and- she-just
-finished- dusting.

-A. Rosebud

THIS POEM IS INSPIRED BY MARIA.

Be A Blessing

You always say that
you are crazy,
but you know what–
I think you are amazing.

I think the truth is,
the dimension you are in is
just so damn, loud
and sometimes you wish
you could turn it down.
It might drive you crazy,
but you are not.
You are sound.

This world was never
meant to change you,
you were meant to
change it,
and you will,
just by being you,
a TRUE blessing.
You are a gift from heaven.

–A. Rosebud

THIS POEM IS INSPIRED BY EMILY TRAFALSKI.

She Rolls Up Her Sleeves

She doesn't give up
when the going gets tough,
she rolls up her sleeves.
You won't catch her
sitting down much because
she's always standing up
for what she believes.
With one fist in the air
and her ear to the streets,
she's never worried about
what she wants,
but what they need.
And they means
anyone who needs a voice.
She'll bring the noise.
She is confident
and a confidant
to anyone who meets her.
You can trust her opinion to be true,
she is not a people pleaser.
She's been down that road before
and she doesn't have time for a detour-
so she is straight to the point.
Like she had wished she had been before,
so many people took advantage of her but
she closed those doors.
She saves up that empathy
and energy
To give to people
she may never meet,
selflessly.
It's a sight to see
she lives life
righteously.
I love her.

A. Rosebud

Living Your Truth Looks Beautiful On You

You built a house with the bricks
people threw at you and
then you threw
a party.
Everyone
who ever mattered
showed up
and for everyone else
- I feel sorry,
because they got an invitation,
but they didn't take it.
To see this stage you are taking.
This is history in the making,
These are stereotypes
you are breaking!
Girl, you are amazing!
And
Love is never perfect,
so just know that
you don't have to be either
No one has to be, to feel it,
to deserve it,
you are worth it.
You are smart
intelligent
beautiful
and kind.
Anyone would
be lucky to have you
in their life.
You are simply the best,
It's no wander why- the world is yelling
#istandwithJESS

A. Rosebud

THIS POEM IS INSPIRED BY KIMBERLY DRAKULIC.

On The Concrete

You left everything that night,
laying there on the concrete.
You no longer had to hear
the screams and cries
from the person who
left -you -there.
You saw the light
and you went towards it.
the warmth that you felt
it was like instantly
you were being held.
God was there
and your life flashed
before your eyes.
You were tired and
you felt like it was your time.
You were ready to accept it
but then came along
the memories of your son
and you thought of
what could become
if you weren't there to
-protect him.
You couldn't let him
feel left and
rejected,
so you BEGGED God
for a second-
chance
and you were resurrected.
Now you are a nurse
and well respected.
You live to help others and
to make them feel accepted.
You are such a blessing.

A.Rosebud

BREAK FREE

After reading everyone's stories,
I started to see one thing in
common-we
all just, want to feel loved......
and not by anyone else,
-but ourselves.
You see, I think we
all need to just
BREAK FREE
from the limits we
set in the web of our minds.
Developed through
trauma and time-
valid but restricting our lives.
How can we-
BREAK FREE,
from the prison inside?
So poisoned
by ego and pride,
we can't admit-
we are tied.
We need to
BREAK FREE
from what we think- we
are supposed to be-
and drop the labels of society.
BREAK FREE
from anxiety,
addiction and
embrace sobriety.
BREAK FREE
from self pity
and feeling like we are
-not enough.
BREAK FREE
from the need to be loved,
by anyone else but ourselves.

-A. Rosebud

CONTRIBUTING PHOTOS INDEX

CONTRIBUTING POETRY, SPOKEN WORD, AND TRAUMA DUMPS

In this section of the book, you will get to read poetry, and spoken word from myself and other women who have contributed their work.

Originally I had only planned to include my own poetry and all of these pictures of these strong and beautiful women, but one of my friends submitted her story and it was just so inspiring I wanted to leave it in complete detail. I thought you would all enjoy this story as well so I asked and she allowed for me to include it in here.

After that, I sent out the word and few other people submitted something and this section began to grow. I am so proud of these women for sharing their stories to inspire others who might be going through something similar. I feel so honored to include their work in this book. This is a dream come true for me to be able to lift up others voices in this way.

Please remember that this is a living work and if you would like to share your story, you can visit our website- GirlDontGiveUp.com to submit your entry for one of our upcoming editions. You can submit anything you want to release. Maybe you want to talk about your childhood, a divorce, a hurtful friend, a health matter.. This is a safe space to express yourself with poetry, spoken word or you can just submit a straight up trauma dump.

By reading similar stories and seeing other people who have been through some of the same traumas that we experience, it helps us to not feel so alone. That's what I want to do. I want you to know, you are not alone.

To My Broken Self:

Do you know what I did
with that broken girl?
The one who had been
attempting to destroy
every single flaw for as long
as she could remember?
That girl who was talking to God,
a God she hadn't believed
would take it away in the beginning.
That girl, the one who couldn't
even look at herself in the mirror,
no self worth and hurting herself everyday.

She started loving herself.
Now telling herself-
I AM OKAY!
I WILL BE OKAY!

I know I need to shut some doors,
especially the ugly ones.
Everyday I try and tell myself
you are perfect as you are.
Remember, you are loved,
nothing is to be feared.
I have learned patience
and to smile more.
You know why?
Because I am beautiful.

-Ashley Derry

I Write

I write because
sometimes
I just don't want to speak.
You see
sometimes me
and the voices in my head-
we just don't agree.
So I'll write it out-
just to see
if it's something I believe
because these voices are
misleading
and sometimes they succeed in
Messing up my whole day.
Sometimes I get so stressed out
over some shit I just
didn't even have to say,
So I write.

A. Rosebud

This is What Nursing Means To Me

Dear God,

Some days I trudge through
the muck and the mire

and I wonder, is this really
my heart's desire?

Other days I actually
reach the end of the maze.

Then once again my heart
is ablaze.

What is this fire, that at times has
me almost crazed?

It is Nursing
It is Life

By: Patricia Jenkins, RN

"Why I Stayed"

M had a handgun that he kept under his mattress at all times. He loved to bring it out when we fought and wave it in my face, even knocking me across the skull with it a few times. But I knew he would never shoot ME; what I was afraid of was him shooting himself. I am not sympathizing with him or defending his actions, but I will admit that he had problems with himself more than with others. This guy had watched his mother get beaten by his father his entire life and, although I could never get him to admit it, I do believe his father had hurt him too. He had anger issues, a past of self-mutilation, and an all-around low self-esteem. I felt bad for him – reason #1 for staying. He was a wounded puppy who just never knew anything other than violence. Whenever I tried to leave, he turned the gun on himself. I was all he had (except, of course, the girl I later found out he was cheating on me with the entire time), and I couldn't bear to be the reason this depressed man took his life.

I will never forget the night I left. He had dropped me off at my house, where I lived with my mother, and we were fighting about something ridiculous – I had probably looked at our waiter the wrong way and, even after I dropped out of high school and quit my passion, dance, for him, he still assumed I was screwing every guy who looked at me. He threw some punches and pushed me onto the cement road, and sped away. My poor mother held me as I cried that night, as she did hundreds of other nights, not knowing how truly bad it was. After she had gone to sleep, M had called me, drunk and angry. We fought and, by some miracle, I found an ounce of bravery inside me and I said "I'm done. We're done. This is the last time I'm saying this." And hung up. Within a minute he called back: "I love you, good bye" followed by the sound of the clicking of the magazine on his gun. He hung up, sent a text message..."BOOM" and then turned his phone off. I lost it, woke my mother up and told her what was going on. She took my phone from me and called his landline. He answered, she told him to leave me alone for good. And that was it. Of course, he stalked me for weeks...waiting outside my house for me to come out so he could beg forgiveness. Texting me apologies, asking mutual friends to talk to me and express how heartbroken he was, how I should give him another chance. But I was free from him.

Free from the guilt? Not so much. No, I don't mean I blame myself for the abuse in a "I didn't obey him, I deserved it" kind of way. I blamed myself for staying. I blamed myself for letting him have that much control over my life for so long. I look back and think about how pathetic I was for dropping out of school and leaving what I was most passionate about because HE TOLD ME TO. I was embarrassed of my weakness. I am a strong, independent woman, a raging feminist...how did I let it get that far? Why didn't I just leave!? Well, then I think of the night I did leave. The night I thought I was about to be responsible for someone's suicide.

I did try to leave another time before that, though. A month earlier his brother had gotten married and we had a pretty good night. He was drunk, happy-dancing-goofy-drunk, talking about how amazing it will be when we get married. I remembered for an hour or so why I fell in love with him in the first place. I, being underage and hoping to keep him happy for a night, offered to be the designated driver. He was letting me drive his car (his most prized possession) so my nerves were on edge. Pulling out of a parking lot I must have hit a pot hole and bottomed out a little bit - he had blue under glow lights and I might have broken them. Happy-drunk-M was gone. Angry-drunk-M was back, and I immediately realized how big of a mistake I had made. He was pissed, no longer wanted to spend the night with me. "Just go to your house, I can't even look at you right now." His rage at that moment was unreal and I had no idea what was in store for me. He screamed in my ears as I drove, swung his hands at me, smacked me across the head like I was a dog who just shit on the carpet.

When I pulled up to the curb in front of my house, I pulled too close and his rims (which, I will never forget, cost him $1200 each) scratched along the cement. At this point I was genuinely afraid for my life. He jumped out of the car and ran around to the driver's side, reached in and, grabbing my hair, screamed in my face about how much of a fuck-up I was. He then pulled me out of his car and onto the pavement, and sped away (this was a common theme...his car made him feel powerful). I went inside and cried to my mom and, of course, he returned to play the hero. "Baby, I'm so sorry about our fight. I love you."

He slept with me that night and in the morning drove us to his house where I left my car the day before. The next thing I know, we're fighting again and I'm transferring my things from his car to mine. I handed him a bouquet that belonged to his sister from the night before, which had a needle sticking out of it, I guess. The needle cut his hand and he flipped. I was so scared. I just jumped in my car and began driving home.

He followed me in his car on the road that traveled between his house and mine, a long twisty hellish road. He rode the ass of my car and I was shaking, scared for my life. I wanted nothing more than to be done with all of it. So I went around a bend and ran head-on into a tree, wholly on purpose. That was the week I left school and quit dance. That was when I realized...there was no way to leave. I was stuck.

Still, there are days I hate myself and I blame myself for being scared. My fear is my fault. I was weak. I was the coward. I could have done something but I didn't.

But all the other days, I'm only aware of my strength. I look at that as just another obstacle I've faced and conquered. I add it to the list of reasons I can survive.

"Why I Stayed."
-Anonymous

Unanswered Questions

I have so much on my mind,
I didn't get to say to you.
You were my best friend and my worst enemy.
You know what they say is true.
The apple doesn't
fall far from the tree, but I tried,
I can't help it- I am still
so much like you, on the inside.
You know you really hurt me, when you died.
I know that sounds selfish, but mom, you lied

You said you got help, on the inside.
You made me tell the judge,
you'd be within -my eye.
But now you're only there when I cry.
You ditched me! I came to pick you up,
I got the kids ready. I saw you!
I saw you there, right where
I promised you I would be-
and you saw me- but you hurriedly
took another ride home.
As much as I blame you,
I blame myself-
for leaving you alone.
Mom, I was tired of the shit,
Selfish. I know.
Now I have so many
unanswered questions,
Like- where is your phone, mom?
Where did it go?
Who gave you the drugs, mom?
Was it someone I know?
Did somebody hurt you,
was this on your own?
Was this on purpose
or a random- overdose?
I'll guess I'll never know.

Anonymous

Putting Yourself Back Together

Sometimes it takes things
to fall apart for better things
to fall into place.
Sometimes it takes
the most uncomfortable path
to lead your life to
the most beautiful place.
You'll never see that purpose
of someone leaving your life
until you see it was best for your life.
You'll never understand why
you went through it until
you see the strength,
power and resilience
that it built inside of you.
Your current situation
is not your final destination.
Just because something is over,
doesn't mean your life is over.
The pain you conquered though
will be pain of the past.
The fear that you are experiencing
will soon turn into the fear you have overcome.
This chapter is not your story,
this moment is not your identity,
and this pain is not your life.
The tables in your life will turn,
pain will become power,
weakness will become strength,
and confusion will be peace.
Better things are coming,
everyday is a new beginning,
treat it that way.

-Ashley Derry

Time

The only thing that separates
Life from death is time.
Time has the power to make
A crooked man, straight
An early man, late
A loving man, hate.
Time flies and calls
But it doesn't wait
And we all just need more of it.
Don't we???
Time is thought to be an illusion
But I believe on Earth it is real.
I've come to this conclusion
Because it takes TIME to heal
The Bible says in the beginning
God created light- but
read that again-
there was a beginning, right?
So time already existed
The quantum realm
and the 4th dimension
coexisting.
If you have ears that hear
I need you to listen.
Time is the most valuable resource
You will ever be gifted.

Spend if wisely.

A. Rosebud

What is Real?

I turn on the shower and let it run
until the water is burning like the sun
it's too hot.
I touch it
But I don't feel the pain
Until it registers in my brain
Like "Woah, that's too hot!"
I Pull my hand away
that pain must be real
but what if it's not?

You see what if everything around us
is just a manifestation of our thoughts

What if we could manipulate
the thought waves
on a larger scale
to create a big change-
Let's take
what we think to be middle age
for instance,
We all say it's 40 right
but what if we just didn't?
What if we said it was 80?
What if our conscience shifted
and our lifespans doubled
in an instant?

I get it,
I'm gonna lose some of y'all here
but for those of you
with ears to hear
I want you to listen....

Continued on to next page-

Our thoughts create our reality
and our reality is our existence
and our existence exists in
this equation
in the quantum realm
that creates all of the substance
around us
based on
our thoughts.

It's like you put your thoughts
into the universe
like you put your question
into a google search
and wait for the results.
Sometimes the answer
is not what you are expecting
but the problem is always solved.

Are you with me?
You see-
My father went on a trip one time
and while he was trippin
he looked up at the moon and
there was this, string like thing
coming from his belly button
like an umbilical cord
and his cord, attached to the moon, that
attached to the sun, that attached to the
earth and
all living things on our planet.
He said, the way
that he could understand it
we are all on this, universal grid
and we all
contribute to it
like the World Wide Web
Are you following me?

-Anonymous

It'll Be OK Babygirl

As women, we strive for perfection
thinking it's a worthier calling
then the journey we are on.

You try so hard your entire life
to be the good girl,
the one everyone expected.

Fixing everything that was bad
about you or doing it all right
isn't what it is about;

Reclaiming everything you lost
is what it is about.
Returning to a wholeness.

Remember:
You are worthy simply because you exist.

–Ashley Derry

"Everything that ever was,
ever is and ever will be-
is in the universe at one time.
Right now.
In this moment.
It already exists.
Everything-accessible-
at one time,
like a hard drive.
Your experience is the
one you are thinking or
choosing to access."

-A. Rosebud

To everyone who contributed to the success of this book, thank you so much. From the pictures, to the poetry, to the stories, to watching my children so that I can spend some time focussing on completing this book- THANK YOU!

This has been such an honor.

Don't forget, this book is a living work which means that more copies of this book will be created in the future with additional pictures, poetry and written word. If you are interested in submitting a photo of yourself or your story to be included in our next edition-

visit GirlDontGiveUp.com
and submit your entry today.

I would love to hear your story and include you in the next one!

Again- thank you so much to everyone who has contributed to this book. You are all amazing and without your bravery, this wouldn't have been possible. Keep on going, keep on growing and
Girl, Don't Give Up.

Follow the author on social media to stay up to date on future book releases, opportunities to collaborate or to reach out for any reason at all:

TikTok.com/AliciaRosebud

YouTube.com/EatPrayHustle

Facebook.com/AliciaRosebud

Instagram.com/BossLady_Jenkins

Instagram.com/ARosebudPoetry

Made in the USA
Columbia, SC
29 October 2021